The
GREATEST
DINOSAUR
EVER

BRENDA Z. GUIBERSON

Illustrated by
GENNADY SPIRIN

HENRY HOLT AND COMPANY
NEW YORK

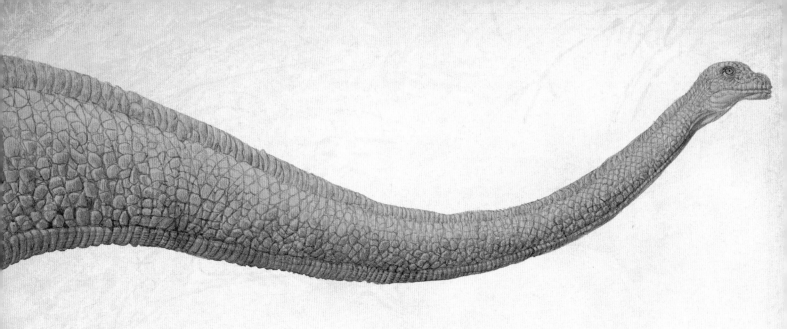

With thanks and appreciation to Laura Godwin
for her creative dinosaur inspiration, and to Kate Butler, Patrick Collins,
George Wen, and Marianne Cohen for such thoughtful input.
—B. Z. G.

Henry Holt and Company, LLC
Publishers since 1866
175 Fifth Avenue
New York, New York 10010
mackids.com

Library of Congress Cataloging-in-Publication Data
Guiberson, Brenda Z.
The greatest dinosaur ever / Brenda Guiberson ; illustrated by Gennady Spirin.
pages   cm
Includes bibliographical references.
Audience: 4–8
ISBN 978-0-8050-9625-5 (hardcover)
1. Dinosaurs—Juvenile literature. 2. Dinosaurs—Pictorial works—Juvenile literature. I. Spirin, Gennady, illustrator. II. Title.
QE861.5.G85 2013   567.9—dc23   2013001725

Henry Holt books may be purchased for business or promotional use.
For information on bulk purchases please contact Macmillan Corporate and Premium Sales Department at
(800) 221-7945 x5442 or by e-mail at specialmarkets@macmillan.com.

First Edition—2013 / Designed by Patrick Collins
The artist used oil paint on paper to create the illustrations for this book.
Printed in China by South China Printing Co. Ltd., Dongguan City, Guangdong Province

1 3 5 7 9 10 8 6 4 2

To Jason,
who first infused me with wonder and passion
for the greatest dinosaurs ever
—B. Z. G.

To my beloved grandson
—G. S.

Who was the greatest dinosaur that ever lived?

I was the greatest. I was the tallest and the biggest herbivore. I had a long neck with the highest reach into the trees. The earth shook when I walked.

I, SAUROPOSEIDON,

(SORE-oh-po-SY-don)

was the greatest dinosaur of them all!

I was the greatest. I was the longest carnivore,
even longer than Giganotosaurus. And I had a
beautiful sail-like crest on my back.

I, SPINOSAURUS,

(spine-oh-SORE-us)

was the greatest dinosaur of them all!

I was the greatest. I was the strongest. I had the longest teeth that could bite right through meat and bone. With a single crunch, I could crush and swallow 500 pounds of food.

I, TYRANNOSAURUS REX,

(ti-RAN-oh-SORE-us rex)

was the greatest dinosaur of them all!

I was the greatest. I had weird, gigantic arms and could cut down plants with my three-foot-long claws. My big potbelly could digest all the tough food I ate.

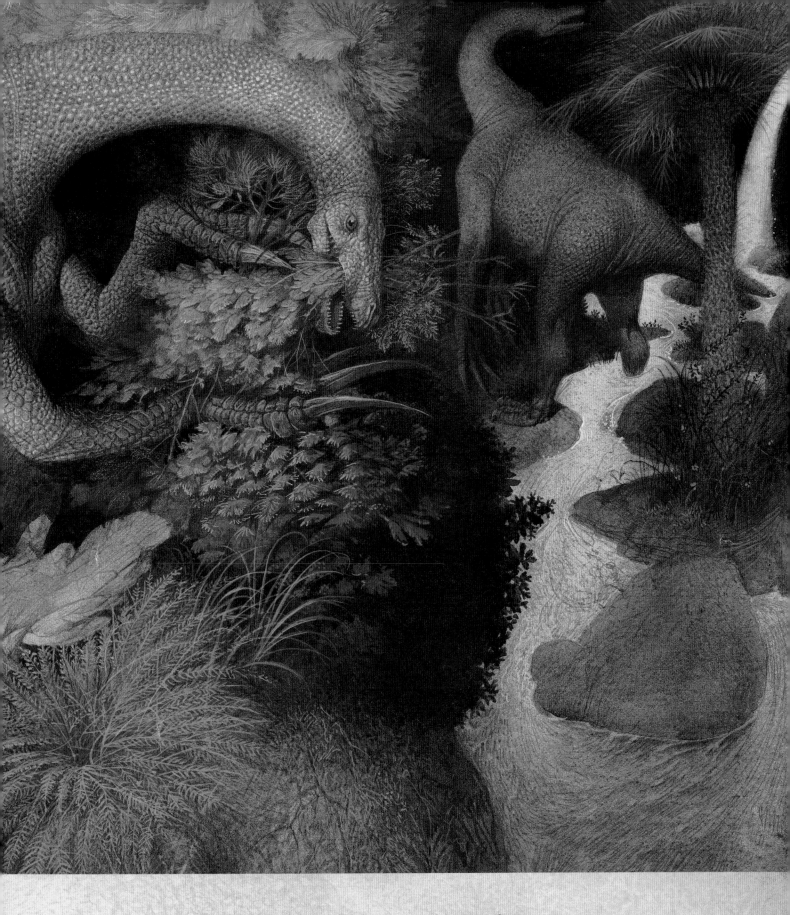

I, THERIZINOSAURUS,

(THER-ih-ZIN-oh-SORE-us)

was the greatest dinosaur of them all!

I was the greatest. I had the longest spikes at the end of my tail. They were sharp and strong and as long as a third grader. On my back I had 17 stunning plates shaped like kites.

I, STEGOSAURUS,

(STEG-uh-SORE-us)

was the greatest dinosaur of them all!

I was the greatest. I had the best armor. My body was covered with bony plates, spikes, and horns. There was a club on my tail that could swing like a whip. I even had armored eyelids to protect my eyes.

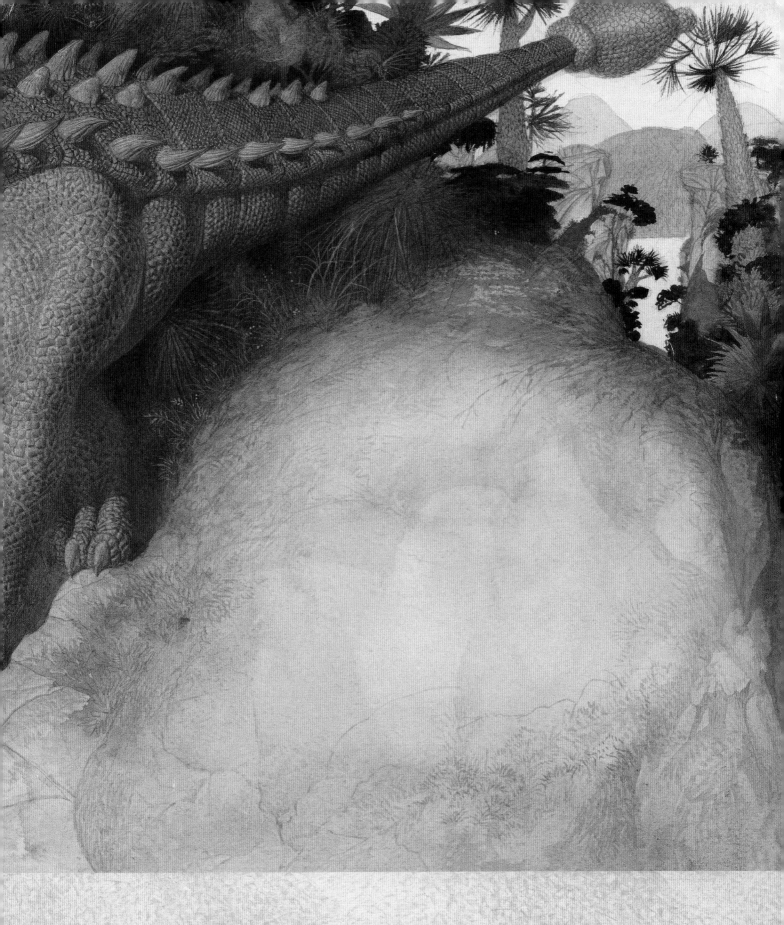

I, ANKYLOSAURUS,

(AN-ki-loh-SORE-us)

was the greatest dinosaur of them all!

I was the greatest. I was the fastest and could run over 40 miles per hour. I had lightweight hollow bones for extra speed and a long tail to keep my balance.

I, ORNITHOMIMUS,

(or-nith-oh-MIME-us)

was the greatest dinosaur of them all!

I was the greatest. I was the smartest. I had the largest brain for my size and was smarter even than the mammals that lived around me. With large eyes and extra brainpower, I could spot creatures hiding in the shadows and hunt when it was dark.

I, TROODON,

(TROH-oh-don)

was the greatest dinosaur of them all!

I was the greatest. I had the best night vision. I lived close to Antarctica in a cold forest. I could see well during the dark winter months when the sun did not appear.

I, LEAELLYNASAURA,
(lee-EL-in-ah-SORE-ah)

was the greatest dinosaur of them all!

I was the greatest. I was the first dinosaur to say I was a bird. Like modern birds I had feathers, hollow bones, and even a wishbone. I was just learning to fly.

I, ARCHAEOPTERYX,

(ark-ee-OP-ter-icks)

was the greatest dinosaur of them all!

I was the greatest. I was the best parent. While some
dinosaurs left their eggs behind, I built a three-foot
nest and carefully filled it with eggs. Then I plopped
down over the eggs and protected them.

I, OVIRAPTOR,

(OH-vi-rap-ter)

was the greatest dinosaur of them all!

I was the greatest. I was the smallest. I had sharp claws to climb trees. I had long flight feathers on both my arms and legs. With four feathered wings, I could glide from tree to tree and had clever ways to survive in a world of giants.

I, MICRORAPTOR,

(MY-crow-rap-ter)

was the greatest dinosaur of them all!

So which dinosaur was the greatest?

Was it the tallest, the biggest, the strongest, the smartest, the weirdest, the fastest, or the smallest? Or was it the oldest bird, the best parent, the one with the best night vision, the toughest armor, or the longest tail spikes?

Or could it be a dinosaur still waiting for discovery— the greatest dinosaur ever?

You decide!

Dinosaurs of the World

SAUROPOSEIDON
"earthquake god lizard"

PRONUNCIATION: SORE-oh-po-SY-don

SIZE: 98 feet long, head could reach 56 feet into the air

PERIOD: Early Cretaceous, 112 million years ago

LOCATION: Oklahoma

SPINOSAURUS
"spine lizard"

PRONUNCIATION: spine-oh-SORE-us

SIZE: 47 feet long

PERIOD: Cretaceous, 100–93 million years ago

LOCATION: North Africa

TYRANNOSAURUS REX
"tyrant lizard king"

PRONUNCIATION: ti-RAN-oh-SORE-us rex

SIZE: 42 feet long, 6 tons

PERIOD: Late Cretaceous, 70–65 million years ago

LOCATION: USA, Canada

THERIZINOSAURUS
"reaping lizard," also "scythe lizard"

PRONUNCIATION: THER-ih-ZIN-oh-SORE-us

SIZE: 33 feet long, 5 to 6 tons

PERIOD: Late Cretaceous, 83–70 million years ago

LOCATION: Mongolia, China

STEGOSAURUS
"roof lizard"

PRONUNCIATION: STEG-uh-SORE-us

SIZE: 30 feet long

PERIOD: Late Jurassic, 155–145 million years ago

LOCATION: Western USA, Europe

ANKYLOSAURUS
"fused lizard"

PRONUNCIATION: AN-ki–loh-SORE-us

SIZE: 25–35 feet long

PERIOD: Late Cretaceous, 70–65 million years ago

LOCATION: USA, Canada

ORNITHOMIMUS
"bird mimic"

PRONUNCIATION:
or-nith-oh-MIME-us

SIZE: 15 feet long

PERIOD: Late Creta-
ceous, 76–65 million
years ago

LOCATION: Western
USA, Canada

ARCHAEOPTERYX
"ancient wing"

PRONUNCIATION: ark-ee-OP-ter-icks

SIZE: crow size, 18-inch wingspan

PERIOD: Late Jurassic, 151–145 million
years ago

LOCATION: Germany

TROODON
"wounding tooth"

PRONUNCIATION: TROH-oh-don

SIZE: 6 feet long, 100 pounds

PERIOD: Late Cretaceous, 76 million years ago

LOCATION: USA, Canada

OVIRAPTOR
"egg thief"

PRONUNCIATION:
OH-vi-rap-ter

SIZE: 8 feet long,
77 pounds

PERIOD: Late
Cretaceous, 70
million years ago

LOCATION: Mongolia,
China

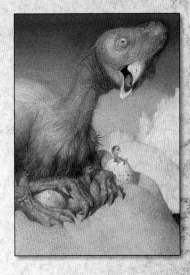

LEAELLYNASAURA
"Leaellyn's lizard"

PRONUNCIATION:
lee-EL-in-ah-SORE-ah

SIZE: 8 feet long,
25 pounds

PERIOD: Early Cretaceous,
106 million years ago

LOCATION: Australia

MICRORAPTOR
"little thief"

PRONUNCIATION:
MY-crow-rap-ter

SIZE: hawk size,
12 ounces

PERIOD: Early
Cretaceous,
124 million
years ago

LOCATION: China